Collydean Primary School
Glenrothes

ANDY'S
BIG QUESTION

Where do I belong?

A Child's Guide to Adoption

By Carolyn Nystrom
Illustrated by Ann Baum

A LION BOOK
Tring • Batavia • Sydney

Text copyright © 1987 Carolyn Nystrom
This illustrated edition © 1987 Lion Publishing

Published by
Lion Publishing plc
Icknield Way, Tring, Herts, England
ISBN 0 7459 1270 2
Albatross Books Pty Ltd
PO Box 320, Sutherland, NSW 2232, Australia
ISBN 0 86760 872 2

First edition 1987

British Library Cataloguing-in-Publication Data

Nystrom, Carolyn
    Andy's Big Question: where do I belong?
    —— (The Lion Care series)
    I. Title   II. Baum, Ann
    813'.54 [J]   PZ7
    ISBN 0–7459–1270–2

Printed and bound in Belgium

This is Andy. Andy lives in a big old farmhouse in the country. It's not a pretty house. It's not even a comfortable house. It's hot in summer and cold in winter. Even the furniture is old, with threads and springs coming out at odd places. But Andy likes his house because it's the kind of place where you don't have to be careful where you put your feet.

Andy's dad teaches history at a big comprehensive school. In the summer holidays he likes working in the garden. Dad's garden is full of food: tomatoes and marrows and lettuces and beans and potatoes and onions and fruit for pies and sunflowers for birds. Dad teaches all the children to help in the garden. Andy helps too.

Andy's mum works at home. She cleans their big
house once a week. She freezes lots of vegetables
from the garden. She does mountains of washing in
the machine and cooks lovely meals in big saucepans
on the cooker. When Andy's family goes to church
on Sunday, they fill up a whole row.

Lots of children live at Andy's house. Some live there for a long time and some for only a few days. But Andy came to stay. Andy was adopted.

A long time ago, Andy came to this big house with its swing in the oak tree, six cats in the barn, two dogs in the backyard, and lots of room to play and have fun. Andy was only three then. He carried Foofee, his toy dog, and his special blanket called Geegee.

Andy can hardly remember his first mum carrying him up the steps, talking to him excitedly about his new house. When she gave him a final hug and kiss, Andy's cheek was wet with her tears. He touched her eye with one finger and said, 'Sad?'

Some children have several parents. Birth parents are the man and woman who give life to a baby. When a baby begins inside his mother, he is as tiny as a dot on this paper. He is made partly from a birth father and partly from a birth mother.

Foster parents look after a child who has to live apart from his birth parents for a while. But foster children usually still belong to the birth parents. They will probably go back home one day.

Adoptive parents take a child who has no home into their own family. They give this child the same rights as if he had been born to them.

An adoption agency or the Social Services department arranges for children who need a home to be looked after. Social workers from the agency help find foster homes and adoptive homes. Before an adoption is final, social workers check to see if the new family is working well together.

Now Andy is ten. Because his family is a foster family, lots of children come and go. But not everyone leaves. Sara and Laura were born to this family. They are at secondary school now and will live at home until they are grown up.

Andy doesn't look like Sara and Laura. He doesn't look like Mum and Dad either. But he is just as much part of their family. Being adopted means, 'I belong.'

Sometimes Andy is not sure he likes belonging to this busy family. If he thinks really hard he can almost remember his first mum. When he gets angry with Mum and Dad he sometimes thinks he'd rather be with her.

One Tuesday night, Andy was sitting at the long kitchen table with his homework. Dad was marking essays and Mum was washing up. Andy looked out of the window. The dogs lay snoozing in the evening sun. It would soon be dark.

Andy couldn't see why anybody needed to know about a stupid war that happened hundreds of years ago. So he played with his pencil, and looked at the pictures in his book. Finally he closed his book with a loud slap and said, 'I've finished.' Then he scooted out of the back door to play.

Ten minutes later Dad stormed out with Andy's exercise book in his hand.

'Andy, come here,' he bellowed. 'If you did your homework, you wrote in invisible ink. How about doing it again properly? And since you think going out to play is so important, there'll be no more outside play this week!'

Andy felt a red rush of anger building up his back all the way to the top of his head.

'The whole week?' he yelled. 'Just because of one rotten piece of homework?'

He grabbed his homework book and shouted, 'I hate homework. My real mum wouldn't make me do it. I know she wouldn't. I want to go and live with her!' Then he ran into the house, slammed the door, and ran up to his room.

Andy kicked his waste-paper basket. Then he kicked his chest-of-drawers and punched his pillow. After a while he felt the anger prickles fading from his neck. He leaned back against his pillow and stared out of the window.

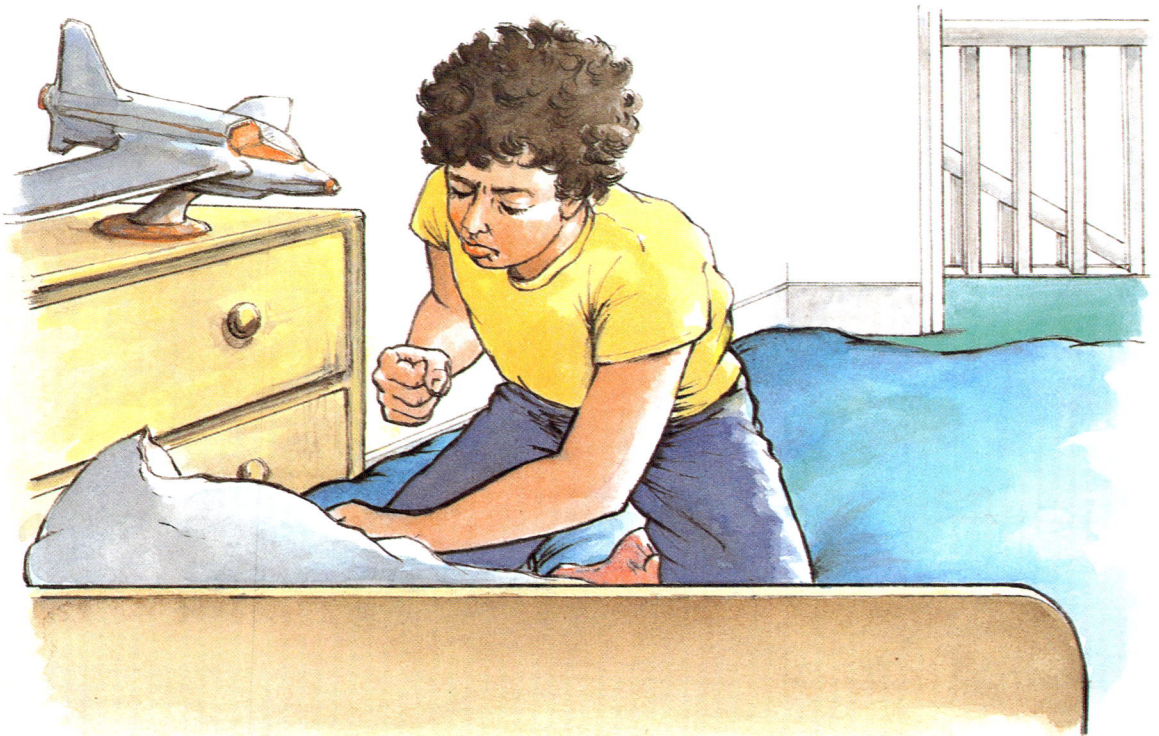

'Why did I get so angry?' Andy wondered. Two things came to mind: school and his mother—not the mum downstairs peeling apples for tomorrow's pies, but his first mum. Just lately it seemed as if every time he thought about school or his first mum, he got in a temper. He got in a temper about school because he never seemed to do as well as Sara and Laura, or even as well as Mum and Dad expected him to. And he got in a temper about Mum— for thousands of reasons, most of which he couldn't spell out.

Later that night, Andy's dad came upstairs and sat next to Andy on his bed. Andy showed Dad the homework he'd now done—all ready for tomorrow. Dad checked each answer as carefully as he checked his own pupils' history essays. Then he put his arm around Andy.
'Do you sometimes miss your first mum?' he asked quietly.
Andy felt a lump in his throat so big that he couldn't talk. He just nodded his head. He wished he could tell his dad the hundred questions that crowded into his mind.

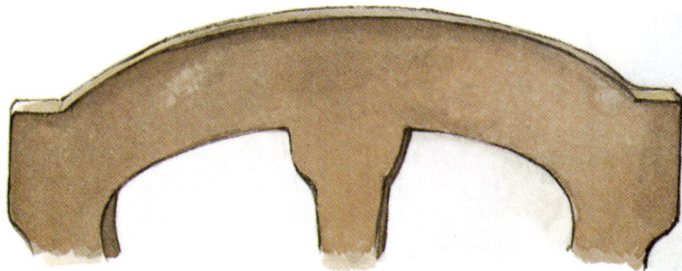

Dad sat still and held him for a while. But when Andy didn't say anything, he left and closed the door. Andy heard his dad's footsteps get softer down each stair. He looked at the smiling faces of his family in the photo propped up on the chest-of-drawers. There he stood between Sara and Laura, with Dad's arm on his shoulder and Mum on the other side. But did he really belong in that smiling group?

Children who are adopted sometimes have a lot of questions about their families. They wonder:

What is my first mother doing now? Does she miss me?

Who was my father before I was born?

Did my first mother have other children? Are they my sisters and brothers?

Who do I look like?

Why did Mum and Dad adopt me?

Do Mum and Dad love the children born to them more than they love me?

If my first mother gave me away, will my new parents give me away too?

Would my mum and dad be upset if they knew how much I think about my first mum?

Could I find my first mother if I tried? Would she want to see me?

But the biggest question many adopted children ask is, 'Why did my first mother give me away?' And behind that question is a nagging crinkle of fear, 'Is there something wrong with me?'

Next morning, the questions felt softer in Andy's mind. He sat down at the long kitchen table and bowed his head while Mum thanked God for the food. Mum had made muesli for breakfast with apples and raisins and brown sugar—Andy's favourite. Andy looked up and down the long table. Except for Sara and Laura with their olive skin and straight black hair, none of the children looked much alike.

Gina was his own age. She had lived with them for six months now, but soon she was going to live with her father and his new wife.

George was living with them just for this school year while he finished his car mechanic's course. Then he would get a job and live on his own.

And banging a spoon noisily on the tray of his highchair was Jules. Jules' mum had left him on his own in their flat one day and never come back. The neighbours had brought him to Andy's house. Mum and Dad didn't know how long Jules would be with them.

Andy helped to feed Jules. Sometimes he made the spoon go round and round Jules' head like an aeroplane before he finally pushed it into his mouth. Then Jules laughed and clapped his hands for more.

Suddenly it was time to go. Everyone scurried round for jackets and books before running down the lane to meet the school bus.

'Thanks for the muesli, Mum,' Andy whispered, as he gave her a quick hug and kiss on his way out of the door.

Maybe being adopted into a family like this wasn't so bad, he decided, as he ran to catch up with Gina.

People adopt children for lots of different reasons. But mostly they adopt because they love children and enjoy the job of being a parent. Parents love an adopted child in the same way as they love their own. Sometimes they get angry, like last night when Dad shouted at Andy for lying about his homework. But teaching a child what is right—and then seeing that he does it—is part of a parent's job.

Will Andy's parents give him away? No. When parents are thinking of adopting a child, they must first look after him in their home for at least six months, maybe even longer. By then they can be sure that they want to keep him until he is grown up. Only then can they go to court to sign adoption papers. Once a child is adopted, the law says he belongs to that family just as much as if he were born there.

Wednesday night is family night at Andy's house. All the children do their homework as soon as they get home from school, and Mum makes an early supper. Nobody watches TV and phone calls have to be short. It is a family time. After supper, they all play games like Monopoly or Happy Families or even football. (Andy likes football best.)

Later, Dad gets his Bible out and all the children who are old enough to read get their Bibles too. Andy's family studies a small part of the Bible together, and they talk about ways they can live by what it teaches.

'Tonight I want to look at what the Bible says about adoption,' Dad began.

Dad didn't look his way, but Andy squirmed anyway. After all, he was the only adopted person in the room. But maybe the Bible would answer some of his questions.

'Did you know that God adopts people into his family?' Dad asked. 'Let's see how he does that.'

Soon everyone was looking at the first paragraphs of the Gospel of John in the New Testament. Andy listened while George read about Jesus coming to the world. One sentence leapt out at him: 'Yet to all who received him, to those who believed in his name, he gave the right to be children of God.'

Those words stuck in Andy's mind. 'The right to be a child of God,' he thought. 'Is that like the right to be a child of Mum and Dad?'

Andy's family talked about it for a while.

'It says here that Jesus came to earth so that people can believe and receive him,' George said thoughtfully.

'And then they become children of God,' Gina announced, with a triumphant look at Andy.

Then Andy spoke up for the first time. 'It looks as if being adopted into God's family is just like being adopted here. It means, "I belong."'

But by Thursday morning Andy's old questions were back as he stared out of the school bus window. 'Who do I look like? Not like Sara or Laura or Mum or Dad. I belong with them, but I don't look like them.'

Andy tested the shadowy memories of his first mother. He couldn't see her face at all in his mind —everyone seemed big and old when he was only three. Andy touched his own curly hair. Maybe her hair was dark and curly too. Without even trying he realized that his eyes were searching the pavement for a woman with dark curly hair and a face like his. 'Maybe if I look every day, I'll find her.' But then he thought, 'I'd feel really silly walking up to every dark-haired lady I meet and asking, "Are you my mother?"'

Adopted children often wonder if they look like their birth parents—and sometimes they do. They may even have some of the same talents as their birth parents.

But adopted children become like their adoptive parents too. They learn what their adoptive families teach them. They may even begin to walk and talk and use hand gestures just like their adoptive parents.

Yet one thing is more important than either set of parents: choice. It's tempting for an adopted person to blame everything he does on something inherited from his birth parents or learned from his adoptive parents. But that's not fair. Almost everything he does, he chooses to do. And he has to take responsibility for his own choices.

Andy is a mixture of all of these things. Andy doesn't know it, but his body looks much like his birth father's. But Andy does his homework after school because his adoptive parents have taught him that homework is important. Andy's choices, however, are his own. Andy chose to lie about his homework. And Andy chose to help feed baby Jules. And Andy even chooses to put tomato sauce on his mashed potatoes.

Thursday dragged by for Andy. A faceless dark-haired woman was at the back of his mind all day. At the end of school, he was trudging out to the bus when he noticed a woman with dark curly hair. She smiled at him from her blue car. Andy stood still for a moment, half turning in her direction. But then a boy came out of school, jumped into the car, gave her a quick hug, and they drove away.

That evening Andy found his homework boring and supper tasteless. George seemed to notice.

'Hey, Andy,' George said, 'do you want a game of football?'

But Andy didn't feel like playing. He just shook his head and climbed the stairs to his room.

Then Andy did something he had not done for a
long time. He burrowed down into the bottom of his
wardrobe and pulled out a bulging pillowcase. Then
he sat cross-legged on his bed and emptied it into his
lap. Out fell a tattered blanket and his old friend
Foofee. Foofee's right front foot dangled by a thread
and stuffing seeped out of a hole in his stomach.

Andy hugged Foofee tightly. If he held the blanket
to his cheek, he could almost smell the flat where he
had lived so long ago with his first mother. He closed
his eyes and tried to see her face, but all he could
remember were her arms holding him. So he just sat
and rocked Foofee for a while.

There was a soft tap on his door. Andy started to shove Foofee back into the pillowcase, but not before Mum stuck her head round the door.

'We're making popcorn . . .' she said, then looked at Andy and came quietly over to his bed and sat down. 'Do you want to talk about what you are thinking?' Mum asked.

Andy nodded.

'I—I think I miss my other mum,' Andy began. He watched Mum's face as she wrinkled her forehead the way she always did when she was worried.

'I mean, I love you and Dad, at least most of the time I do. And I'm glad you adopted me, but I'm scared too. I don't look like Sara or Laura, and I don't do as well in school as they do, either. Do I really belong here?'

While she listened Mum ran her fingers up and down Andy's back the way he liked. But at Andy's question she put her arms round him and held his head next to her shoulder.

'Of course you belong here,' she said. Then she was quiet for a moment.

'Have you noticed that Dad and I aren't much like each other either?'

Andy nodded.

'But we chose each other because of love. Then later we chose you—not because you are exactly like us, but because we love you. And just as we choose to keep on loving each other, even when we disagree, we will also choose to keep on loving you, even when we have problems.'

Andy's eyes strayed to the apple branch outside his window. A lone apple, red and fat from summer sun and rain, waited to be picked before the autumn winds blew it to the ground. His mum watched the apple too, but her eyes were distant as if she were remembering something.

'What are you thinking, Mum?' Andy asked.

'I'm thinking,' his mum began slowly, 'of the time years ago when Dad and I first began talking about whether to adopt a child. We talked about it for a long time. We prayed together about it too. And then you came. Somehow, after that, we often thought of you as a gift from God.'

Andy breathed a deep sigh of relief. 'Then I do belong,' he thought.

Suddenly it felt all right to ask the really hard questions. 'But why did my other mum give me away?' he blurted out. 'Was there something wrong with me? I wonder about the kind of person she was —and if I'm that kind of person too?'

'Your dad and I don't know a lot about your first mother,' Mum said. 'But when you arrived, we learned a little about her. Maybe we can help you with what we learned then . . .' Mum stopped. 'But not now. We need to do some thinking first.'

Then she picked up Foofee. 'Looks as if this fellow needs some repair work. Do you want me to stitch him up?'

Andy nodded. He handed Foofee to Mum and carefully stuffed his blanket back into his pillowcase.

Parents who adopt children sometimes have mixed feelings about birth parents. Because they love the child they adopted, they feel grateful to the man and woman who gave the child life and then allowed them to adopt.

But parents who adopt may also feel a bit afraid of birth parents. They wonder, 'Will my child's first mother come back and try to take my child away?' Birth parents can't do that, because once the adoption is final the child belongs by law to his new family. But the idea is frightening.

And parents who adopt may also feel a bit worried when they think about birth parents. They think, 'What if our child began to love his birth parents so much that he didn't love us any more?' Then the parents would feel sad.

But even though adoptive parents have these mixed feelings about birth parents, they usually understand if their child asks a lot of questions. Even if they don't know much about these parents from the past, most adoptive parents tell their child what they can.

Friday was a new day for Andy. Even though his talk with Mum hadn't really solved any of his questions about his first parents, he felt more settled. On the school bus, he didn't look out of the window for people in the street. Instead, he played magnetic draughts with the boy sitting next to him. And he even got a good mark in his history test. (Must have been all that hard work on the homework questions.) And supper was great: meat loaf, baked potatoes from the garden, and apple pie from their apple tree. It was his turn to wash up, but Laura volunteered to help.

Afterwards, George went back to college to finish a mechanics project. And Mum told Sara and Laura to take Jules outside to play. Suddenly, Andy realized that he was all alone at the kitchen table with Mum and Dad. They both wore their most serious expression.

'Ooops,' thought Andy, 'I think I'm in trouble.'

Dad began. 'Andy, you've been asking a lot of questions lately about your first mum and even about your first dad.'

Andy gulped and nodded.

'We know that you remember your mum a bit, and of course you loved her then. Maybe even now you sometimes miss her.'

Andy nodded again. He was glad they understood at least that much. But he didn't know what to say.

'Your mother and I have worked hard to be good parents,' Dad went on. 'But sometimes we make mistakes. I expect you can remember some of them—like the time we made Gina eat all her peas and she was sick. Then we found out she had got flu,' said Dad. They all laughed. 'All parents are wrong sometimes, so I'm not surprised that you think you might have found a better family somewhere else—maybe even with your first mum.'

Andy looked down at the floor.

Dad continued, 'I think most adopted children ask those kinds of questions. Maybe your first mum knew that too. When you first came to us, she took some time to get to know us. She loved you, you know.'

Andy took a deep breath. 'So why did she give me away?' he asked, his words coming out all in a rush. There it was. The big question lay on the table between them.

'She didn't want to,' replied Andy's mum, joining in. 'That's why she kept you for three years. But taking care of you was hard. Your mum was young when you were born, only seventeen. And she wasn't married.'

Andy looked from Mum to Dad and back again.

Mum continued. 'She tried to make a home for you. She left school so that she could be with you. But later she couldn't get a job. And that meant she didn't have enough money for food or a good place to live. After a while, she began to wonder if she was even being a good mother. It's hard to be a mother when you're not quite grown up yourself.'

Andy remembered all the times Sara or Laura had been his babysitter. It was fun for an evening, but he couldn't imagine them taking over as mum every day.

'. . . she went to an adoption agency.' Dad had now taken over the conversation. 'And that's how you came to us,' he said. 'Your first mum specially asked if you could go to a home where there were other children and where your new parents would teach you about Jesus.'

'At first you were our foster child, just like Gina and George and Jules,' Mum went on. 'But later, your mum decided that she wanted you to grow up in our family. So she asked us to adopt you, and we were so glad.'

'I'm glad too,' Andy said. 'I think.' Then his mind turned to another subject. 'What about my dad?' he asked. 'Do you know anything about him?'

'Only that he was young too, and that he went away to college.' Dad stopped as if remembering, then he added, 'She did say he was the best footballer in their school!'

Andy grinned.

Many adopted children don't know anything about their birth mother or father. But many parents who decide to give their children to another family love their children very much. Giving them away is a hard decision. A woman wants what is best for her child. Finally she decides that her child will have a better life with another family. Her reasons may be much like those of Andy's first mum: no job, no house, no money, no husband.

A child's father may also help decide if the child should be adopted, even if he is not married to the mother. And he too may miss his child when it is gone.

Hard as it may seem, not all parents are able to love their children. They may have been so badly treated themselves when they were young that they have no idea how to love and care for a child of their own. That doesn't mean that there is something wrong with the child—only that he needs a different family where he can learn love. So the child is given to an adoptive family.

It doesn't much matter why a child was adopted. That's all part of the past. More important is the present. Right now, while he is living with his adoptive family, it's best to become as much a part of that family as possible.

Quietly, Andy asked, 'What did my first mum look like?'

Mum handed Andy an envelope. 'I think you're ready for this,' she said.

The envelope was old and crinkled, as if it had spent a long time in the bottom of a drawer. Inside, Andy found a picture and a small curl of dark hair tied with blue wool. The photo showed a young girl, just a bit older than Sara. She held a little boy of about three. The boy's chubby arms clung round her neck, their heads close together, each as dark and curly as the other. Was the lock of hair his, or his mother's? It didn't matter.

That night Andy curled up with Foofee. Mum had sewn him up so that he wasn't falling apart any more —he just looked a bit funny in the mended places.

Before he climbed into bed, Andy put the picture of his first mum next to last year's Christmas picture of his own family, his real family. Then he laid the curl of hair between them.

Some of his questions had found answers. Others would come back without any answers. Perhaps he would think of new and harder questions. But inside he knew, 'This is my family now. This is where I belong.'